THE BOOK OF THE GARDEN

THE BOOK OF
THE GARDEN

RICHARD WEHRMAN

Merlinwood Books · East Bloomfield, NY

Merlinwood Books
PO Box 146
E. Bloomfield, NY 14443

First edition published in 2014 by Merlinwood Books.
Printed in the United States of America.

Drawings by Richard Wehrman

ISBN: 978-0-9913882-0-2

For Barbara Vincent,
who dwells within
the Garden

TABLE OF CONTENTS

THE GARDEN

1

When the searching died away,
and the days grew long
with distractions, with following
blind alleys simply to keep
the feet moving and the mind
away from the dilemma,

then it was that the silence resettled,
and the dried leaves piled up
in the cement corners, one atop the other.
The white heat from the stucco
and the emptiness of the dry fountains
were fine as a memory

but my ear was drawn by
the green sound of water falling
over hidden stones, and the scent of
roses and mock orange, toward feminine
laughter, a speech like flocks of
water-birds whispering

and there was such contentment to lie,
half-concealed by the leaves, under the blue sky
where the clouds billowed white
and passed beneath the sun,
opening veils over the hillside, welcoming the stars
and the warmth of evening's heaven.

One could step, I discovered, into
one's imagination and desire as though
to a place, a world, a physical thing,
and describe it from there, in
a traveler's notebook
of love made manifest—

how the gate glowed
and the path began right there,
on the other side of the fence, at
the property's edge,
and rose through the weeds
up the hill, paved and elusive

with pears on one side
and apples on the other.
The sun was hot and dry, and
the late July afternoon called the
insects on a honeyed wind.
Remnants of white marble eroded

and covered my fingers with chalk;
I lay down, owner and trespasser,
interloper in earth's dream of space,
feeling beneath me the deep layers of pine
needles, hickory nuts and bones, holding
me up, singing me home.

3

Stepping through the gate there
was no gate. The path began where my
foot fell, the gravel raked clean
with one golden leaf for effect
where it settled, pulling me inward
out of the shadows

and each step was a summer, a cycle,
a turning about of a bee or a bird, a sound
sliding down a branch, the bark peeling
into unexplored beauty, as ants shining
in gold wound like a ribbon revolving
about the tree, growing

into the next moment. A fawn, flitting
unseen, a fragment of gold curling, the flash
of bare flesh—a shoulder, a twist—then
the fur of a fox—red—blue with the blood of
a bird dripping fire. The leaves blew
upward in the wind, laughing

as they moved—regal—king and queen
of the unseen, just ahead on the path where
one more step, stopped, was resumed only to settle,
arrested, assaulted by scent, by the sweetness of evening,
by the turn of the year to the flame of the stars,
kissing me, incandescent.

4

Even before the words begin
I can feel the pull, the flow forward,
the invitation in to the green goldness,
as though all barriers to my own being
did not exist, as though a home
had been built for me, and it was the world.

I sat in the center of the garden, and
wherever I stopped on my slow
wandering *was* the center. I gazed over
the sun-shimmering summer heat,
and asked myself, the flowers, the grass:
Why did I walk by? Why did I not come in?

Some days I would miss my books, their
grand ideas, their maps of foreign lands.
And I could read them all, for my diversion,
in the high clouds, in the blue sky.
Hour after hour I would watch the sweet pea
climb from the earth, the apple blossom open.

Evening gave me an indigo cloak. I had
my own stars to echo those singing in the night sky.
I slept with the beetle and the blue black ant;
soft-winged moths settled over my eyes.
The wind breathed on my body: we all
sat together watching the rising moon.

It was dark and the middle of the night,
in the cold times when we lived within walled rooms,
when we made fires to keep warm, before
I knew I lived inside a star. The room
was cold and dark and I missed you, I needed
you. It was silent and I did not know your name.

Not knowing, you moved around me. Not
recognized, you whispered in my ear, you
stroked my body, you caressed me in the night.
I moved in the midst of you, I swam in your
being, I walked everywhere desiring you—yet I
was blind, I reached through you for anything else.

The child, laughing, reaches upward, trying
to grasp the sky, the invisible being.
I am the breath of you," there at the body's
beginning, moving in and out like the tides,
intimate and unknown, lover at the depths,
reluctant to leave, fingers touching—until the end.

How long had the wind and I been lovers? How
long until my petals of ice fell, sheath by sheath
until I saw, I felt, I opened—embraced as I
had always been. How long had no meaning in
our spiral of being, dance of the wind, song
of the wind: our heart's love unending.

6

I am in the garden, yet *I* am not here.
Entire, eden flows about me, radiant
emptiness its source, radiant *my self*
its source, yet no one, no self is here.
Who has wandered here, spreading this garden?
I am dazzled by the sun, overwhelmed by the blue sky.

Try to find me! Your hand passes
through me, I laugh with you in the
yellow flowers! We spin into bees and spiders,
we dart in and out of the apple blossoms,
butterflies dancing in the sun. You cannot find me,
for everything I am is not here!

In the afternoon, having dozed in the
shade, I start awake. Has someone called
my name? I seem to remember a name,
a young boy straying too far from his
mother. I listen but only hear the wind.
A cloud passes overhead, and I begin to be afraid.

"Who am I," I think, "with no one to
name me?" And the wind pushes at my back,
the sun presses against my face. *"You were
beginning to leave us,"* they said, as the stone
pressed into my hand relaxing me, *"and there is
nowhere else for you to go."*

7

The pendulum swings on its gold chain,
back and forth, back and forth. An old man
draws it from his robe, from somewhere inside,
from a slash of red velvet. He is an
old man with white hair, with a white beard.
Wrinkles line his face, and I am a child.

"An old man once gave me this," I tell the boy
who is myself, as the pendulum moves over its shadow,
tracing itself into the moment, as the ravens
watch the old man, as the boy takes it in his hand,
as he leans in to hear its voice whisper
what is true, what is false.

The hanging stone glints in the sun, its tip almost
touching the grass, as the wind lets it lay,
moving within itself. Day spirals about it, stars
bend from beyond the sky to pull upon it,
waters yearn to drink of it, iron in the earth
calls to it: *"Come home, stone, come home."*

I sit in the garden on a wooden bench.
My dark hair is bleached white, the hair of
an old man. I close my eyes, and the trees
and flowers fall away inside me—spreading
my arms I fall away too. In the warm sunlight,
only the pendulum swings.

8

Is it another day, or the same day?
I sleep and I wake, the sun shines and
the moon and stars make their appearance.
The sun is bright in the east; beyond
the pines snow and ice lie everywhere.
Here I am warm among the blossoms.

Have I divided myself in two, I wonder?
All I did was follow the scent of the roses,
the trill of the birds, the buzz of the bees.
On this side, all is the warmth, the beauty
of the garden. On that side, just past the edge,
all I can see is greyness and white ice.

Sitting at the fountain, I gaze at my reflection
in the turquoise water. Through the ripples,
past the moving clouds, I seem to be
all here, all of me. But something
is missing: my anxiety, the old fears,
my opinions. They live outside, in the ice.

I go back to the edge—I go to talk to my old
selves: "Why do you not join me in here,
where it is so much warmer?" *"We cannot
live in such warmth, in the presence of beauty.
We would dissolve,"* they say, *"in what
we are not."*

9

The evening sky is vermillion, is alizarin
clear as diamond. The colors are echoes of
those I have and do love—eyes of the real reflected
in the real. We mingle, we speak, we lace fingers
one with the other; we fade as the colors fade,
we kiss and withdraw.

The first stars light the indigo horizon,
I wander as my evening loves dissolve.
"We are a rare wine," I whisper to them and
to no one, *"we are a gift greater than
all the seven seas."* The moon rises, a
clear crescent, in the reflection of my eye.

Night birds fall silent, a gentle wind
flows in like a tide. My body outspread upon the
grass, the earth hums a song of transformation.
Stars rise across the edges of the field, over
the black row of pines. Drop by drop the air
condenses, as I slowly evaporate into space.

An owl's shadow glides by on dark wings
bringing me back, blinking into earth's blackness.
Silence wraps me: a blanket of all those the Dead love,
whose love forms me. Overhead, the universe
spreads its infinite display: crystal jewels
catch fire across the sky.

+

We row out upon an ocean
of stars. A black pearl drops in the water,
rippling the entire night sky.

+

Overnight the garden creeps into my bedroom.
I see it in the folded covers on the bed, the
wrinkles on the pillows. The soft light
from the window lays with love over everything:
the small spiral notebook, the laptop on the desk.
This unruly garden runs everywhere!

Yesterday outside was outside, and inside
was *in here*, with everything I love. Today
beauty has escaped from the garden. It
infiltrates the plastic gooseneck lamp, it rests
in the shadows of a stone on my bookshelf.
Beauty is a spring flowing everywhere.

The paths from the garden stretch over the field,
through the yard, over the wet snow into the house,
right up to my chair. Flowered vines and tendrils
run rampant, every boundary is breached.
I thought of you as a book I could open and
close when I wished—but you are uncontainable!

Like an undiscovered ruin, you grow over,
you hide the past with your greenness.
Beneath lie the empty walls of old ideas and
crumbled dungeons. In the basement skeletons dance,
banging on drums and cymbals. Spring
is arriving and will not be denied!

11

The morning arrives as love.
On my way to the garden, all things
greet me *as* the garden. The angel sits
on her white stone pillar, waiting where
she appeared yesterday: silent, flaming with light
like a river, radiant, shifting in the wind.

The pillar is waist high, white stone made of
shells from the sea. The angel is attendant, an
announcement, the presence of the Presence—
as are the leaves, the grass, the weathered boards
of the shed. My hand passes through her,
warmed by the sun.

I pass by, present to her presence, as she is
to mine. Words divide us—we are
intimate to each other; *our* intimacy
knows no other. Without desire for what
we are not, we greet each other as our self,
as the Garden, as the World.

The garden spirals inward. it pulls at its
periphery: what seems outside is drawn in.
All edges are erased; that which seemed
dead comes continually into bloom.
Here we are all reflections who reclaim their
actuality, loving our reflections as *our self.*

12

The white wind whips a late snow into
a blizzard: it blows and breathes, blows
and breathes. The windows are iced around the
edges, snowflakes spatter the glass pane.
Such fierceness strips away our pretense—
we grab anything solid and hold on.

Within, the white wind is warm, sustaining,
embracing. Her roar—a lover's whispered words—
rise out of quietness and silence: I mistook
them for absence. She is back—never having
left—showing her irresistibility, the stone
wall of her strength, the white heat of her love.

The wind burns her kisses into me, each
white crystal melts on arrival. She presses
me against the door, she searches inside me.
She penetrates my coat, my gloves, my hat,
reaching everywhere, furious for my body.
We tumble and drift—we bloom, *the white rose*.

Morning brings rest from desire. The whispering
wind has risen, higher, riding over the world of *us*.
A shovel scrapes, reaching under the whiteness
to the bare earth, the solid ground. Slowly
purity is cleared away, a path through what
loves us absolutely, shoveled aside.

13

He sits on a stone bench in the garden.
A full moon rises above the cherry blossoms,
as swallows dart above the dark silhouette
of the trees. Yesterday's snow is only
a memory fading into the night's warmth.
The thin crimson clouds flare, then turn grey.

On his back he gazes up at the first stars.
Why, he wonders, does his heart go back to
his childhood, to the years when life opened
before him, to what he could be, to whom
he might love? He remembers his long walks
after sunset and before dark—

There he wandered city streets, loving the
fading light on the old red brick buildings, the
colors of the sky reflecting from their windows.
It was as though they were a song, a music,
an aroma remembered, that ran like a river,
underground and unseen, but

surfacing in dreams, behind the veil of
the present: here in the grass, the flowers
around him. It was they—here now— who built
this garden, who drew him here, who disguised
themselves as memories, who were none
other than his love, his own sweet heart.

The garden runs like a river, it carries
everything to me, it carries all of it away.
I gaze into the rippling greenness, into the
flowering flow. It is the crumpled cigarette
pack in the gutter, the flattened soda can
shining, the bits of broken glass—

It is the bird's wing, without the bird.
It is the gravel of civilization, it is last
years' leaves. It is the flower petals on
the tree and the dirt under my foot. It is
the stones on the sole of my shoe, my
hand lacing my boot.

It is not an *it* but an *all*, it is everything:
it is the garden, it is the river, it is my
body, it is the wide blue sky. The garden
is voracious, whatever *is* it enfolds.
Spreading over the earth, it confines itself
to my boundaries. It is here, everywhere.

I stop on the path, a small green snake coils
between my feet. The air is warm and I breath
deeply of young oats and clover. Closing my eyes
I am a red swirling river, alive to the sounds of birds
and the buzzing bees. Someone is loving me,
as though I am completely their own.

15

Today old friends are back: the wind
moving through the bare branches, the cold air
once again below freezing, the rose quartz
in my hand—the vibration of my heart.
The trees sway against the grey sky and
I am wrapped in the warmth of the garden.

My heart-wind, my love-wind, carries me
in the six directions. I am the wind
flowing over the earth. I lift and I look,
particles swirl within me: I raise birds and
insects, molecules, dried particles of
men, plants, waters, earth-sifted stardust.

Rose quartz relaxes as I sink into
pink translucence. I am its fractures, its
reflections and depth, its always changing
light. I am alive—never a *rock,* never stone-still.
Within this stone is the garden's completeness.
Touching this stone, I trace my body and soul.

The wind pauses. The trees fall still.
Coldness beholds its clarity—it brings its gift
to spring. Icy sharpness pierces my lassitude and
pulls my eye into preciseness, bringing
my attention to the first green spear, to
the warmth and thrust of Spring.

The garden is sweeping itself clean.
Today the sun is out with a bright clear sky,
and someone has been playing tricks
in the garden. Silk flowers are planted
along the path, as are potted plastic plants
made in China. What is going on here?

Further down the path Christmas lights
are strung looping through the trees. Shiny
plastic stars hang from the low branches.
And further still, laminated cards with
pictures of the Saints flutter
in the morning breeze.

In the distance I catch a glimpse of an
odd fellow dressed in green. Skipping
and jumping he hangs tinsel in the trees.
From somewhere in the weeds a scratchy
record plays Sousa: the drums and horns
of a marching band.

What a clean sweep! What comical sweepers!
My uncluttered garden is now a party house,
a celebration, its own fourth of July. Flowers
explode like firecrackers and confetti. Clapping
hands I surrender—I grab a colored flag and
wave: here comes the band!

17

The late afternoon light is still clear and
bright, casting long shadows from the refuse on
the path. Candy wrappers and curled bits of foil,
spilled popcorn, even a few old love letters.
A good time was had by all, but there's
a lot of cleanup left to do.

Sweeping all the trash into a pile, I
lean on my broom and listen to birds singing
in the bushes and trees. One of them has
begun making a nest with the confetti,
but everyone else has gone home. The garden
welcomes all alike, and smiles when they go.

Clean at last, I welcome the cool breeze
and the first stars. The redbud rubs my
sore back, and I lower myself into the
green grass. When did I become a janitor
to my beautiful garden? I smile and
watch a shooting star arc across the sky.

My old body collects my shovels and broom
and stacks them in our broken down shed.
There's much to repair when spring really arrives.
I turn in slow circles, certain I've forgotten
something, but he's nowhere to be found.
So I wander back to the house for dinner.

Outside the window the sky is a
silvery watercolor grey. Sunlight bleeds into
the edges of the clouds with a white light, and
a gentle breeze stirs the air. A quiet softness
blows through me, touching the love
I hold for the garden.

The quiet silence makes the garden
transparent: it overlays and saturates the
everyday world. Ordinary trees glow,
becoming extraordinary. The first snowdrops
wait beneath last year's leaves, shining with
the light of Persephone, protected by fairies.

Yesterday's circus celebration has moved
out of town, leaving behind a silvered silence
where every sound is a balm, and every
movement is mysterious ecstasy. All the
past gathers in the present moment. Every
love ever loved loves here, within me.

The sun flares white and incandescent, casting
dark shadows. The voice of the wind rises and recedes.
Spring, by the calendar, arrives tomorrow.
But Summer and I reside here in the peace of
the garden. Within my life was saved—
come, let it save yours.

NAMING THE GARDEN

1

Today I am searching for a name: perhaps *the Garden,*
Cold Mountain, or *the Tao—Walden Pond* or
the Pure Land. The name in its exactness escapes
me, like an unbroken wild horse. It gallops
away, leaving only the sound of its hooves,
the smell of the crushed grass.

I feel the desire for a home, an address, a
mailbox on the street. *Homelessness—* is this
the name of my garden? Something wants
to shake me up, loosen my attachments to
everything. A dark face calls me from an alleyway,
a rough voice saying " Give me all you've got!"

Under my feet, it is a new earth arising.
Mountains and rivers of my own naming:
forests and fields arrive for my bedroom, skies
and clouds for my living room and bath.
The basement is a cavern filled with
diamonds and rubies.

The tree by my window tells me to slow down
and relax—any name will do. It is of no importance.
It's like astronomers naming the night sky—
you want to make your fear of the infinite
familiar, when this is the home where you were
born, the everything you already are.

2

Today the unnamed has become
an island, an island of the real.
Everything here knows its true name,
even when it seems as though it doesn't.
You know it instantly—you see
that each particle is real.

The Island—*the Garden*—sits on real ground.
Yet nothing here is holdable. I paddle a small
boat around the island's edges; some days
it is large, other days small. The water doesn't
think the island exists—it will tell you a thousand
reasons why not, enough to drown you.

Feet dangling in the water, I throw small stones
into the lake. "What am I doing?" I think, "I'm
throwing the real into the unreal." Now the
real wraps itself around my toes and ankles.
Its wet warmness says, *"Thank you, thank you.
We are no longer just some idea of yours."*

Later I build a small fire, using the
wood from the large signs I was building,
the ones that said *"The Garden"* and *"The Island"*.
The fire crackles warmly in contentment,
as I add each new piece of wood
to the fire.

3

If you think this garden is some real place
you can go to, you are in error. If you
think the garden is only imaginary, think again.
Few people visit the garden, mainly
birds and small animals, grasses and trees.
Everyone else is like a ghost, barely seen at all.

It's the living who cannot see the garden,
who pass through on their way to somewhere
else. But the Dead visit at every occasion,
wandering the paths, basking in the sunlight
and enjoying the view. These ones who
aren't here anymore—they know what's real.

Today we're giving away free gifts: "Your
Deepest Heart's Desire—Visit the Garden!"
We arrange gold and jewels, framed pictures of
the Beloved. But by late in the day, nobody's come
and we pack them all away. *"Look!"* we say,
pointing to the stars: *"They've come after all!"*

It's no matter, there's no loss or gain.
We're here every day, rain or shine, the garden
and I. Our contentment is as deep as the ocean—we
have more than enough for everyone, and everyone
arrives eventually. And we have all the time
in the World.

4

Overnight the garden has grown itself
a mountain. A miniature mount Fuji rises
into the clouds, and I begin a winding climb,
following paths worn by travelers before me.
At each turn there is a different view—wider
and deeper, more encompassing and beautiful.

Halfway up the mountain I find cast-offs of previous
climbers: rucksacks full of provisions, guidebooks,
canned food, axes and knives. I see sweaters
folded neatly on rocks, a gold bracelet shining in the
sun. It's hard enough to carry one's self up the
mountain. Eventually, you abandon everything.

Closer to the top are small caves in the
mountainside. They are like little nests, with
straw floors and wood stacked for fires. I sit and rest,
gazing from the mouth of a cave. It's easy to relax
here and let go, when all you can see are the white
clouds moving slowly in the blue sky.

The trail ends at the top of the mountain.
Bare and clear, you can see in all directions.
Below is my tiny house and driveway, and the road
that leads up to town. The wind blows hard
against my body, and anything I thought I was
is blown away into the empty sky.

5

The early April sunlight is blinding. Yesterday's
snow is melting, and its reflected light is so brilliant
I must close my eyes: I am flooded in an ocean
of green. Coming down the mountain, I became
filled with uncertainty. Where is the clarity
of the mountain, the surety of the view?

I am on the veranda of a small stone pavilion.
Stairs wind the wall outside from the path below.
I stroke the rust-colored head of a collie,
who has found his way beside me. We stare
into the trees in the garden, where dim
figures dig in the earth below.

Up close, they are like moles or miners.
They wear leather and are covered in dirt. Yet
their hands and faces are facets: emerald and ruby,
sapphire and gold. Their mounds of dirt are
precious stones and silver; their eyes, like mine,
are blinded by the sun.

I no longer know why I am happy or sad,
clear or occluded. The miners keep mining and
piling up stones. I line the garden path with
their handiwork, digging out weeds and setting
stones aligned in the sunlight. My hands and feet
on the path are bathed in reds and blues and greens.

6

After a good night's sleep, I am up again
in the garden. The dog, Ruby, dances around
me, then takes off at a run down the path.
Leaping and barking, she calls me
to follow; near the southern border
she nuzzles in the grass.

On my knees I see a nest made of last year's
twigs and grasses. Bright lights and tiny wings
hover above broken crystal eggshells:
a nest of newborn angels!
They hover and dart, their small voices
a liquid ecstatic choir.

Strange wonders in the Garden! Since when
are angels born like birds or butterflies?
Ruby has no answer, no argument either.
Are these the children of the Angel of the Pillar?
In a dream I am very small, flying in
a golden light with opal wings.

What flying do I need to do with these to lift me?
When grown they guard the cardinal points
and greet me on my daily way. Their hearts
touch my own, and mine theirs—we
rise together breathing into day; our
lips touch, loving the dark night.

7

Today is a melancholy day in the garden. The grey
clouds are low and soft, sounds are hushed,
my feet move slowly down the path. The quiet
is all my own, my friends are made of memory, and
I feel the longing for those I have loved, for new
love to join me as I remember the Dead.

"Your head is telling you stories again." says a
caterpillar climbing a green stem. *"Did you hear
the one about the old man who was going
to die?"* asks a blue jay with a bright eye. "I get
the picture," I tell them all, shaking my head to
empty it. All the real world rushes in.

My dead brother Kenny walks beside me,
sipping his coffee. *"We see with the same eye,"*
he says, *"We taste with the same lips."*
His bright eye gleams like the robin's. His
touch is soft and firm, like the tasseled corn.
Yet I long for his embrace, for our bodies of memories.

There is no answering of anything.
So our Garden is one of delight.
Here every doubt is relieved by things being
just as they are: cherry blossoms in springtime,
wounded hearts in the fall. Soon, as it always does,
everything hidden breaks open into Spring.

8

Some days, the way to the garden is filled
with false starts and difficulties. I end up in thickets
of wild roses, or in the apple tree where hornets
and yellow-jackets make their home.
This trying to get somewhere only
gets me nowhere.

Relaxing, I find the garden where it always is,
around me. I feel the warm sun, I hear the birds
in the trees. There is no need to climb mountains,
discover gold mines, or angels. I am content
to fade away until only contentment
is, and it is the World.

When the garden is cold and wet, it is always
warm and sunny. Where the electric fence crosses
the field, there is no fence at all. As crows
feed on thawed carcass of deer, does and fawns
wander in the grass. Old enemies sip tea
and forget their tired stories, telling new ones.

I am like a baby grasping my mother's finger.
Each beauty of the world, each unknown mystery,
tempts me to hang on. Like the child, my trust
and love brings sleep and contentment,
and curiosity opens my eyes wide,
astonished at the world.

9

A gentle wind arises in the morning.
It has stayed above freezing for three days
in a row, and almost all the snow is gone.
Snow-white and unrepentant, the snowdrops
disregard the frost. What have we to repent,
we who survived this Winter?

The wind, like the grey tatters of cloud,
snatches the garden away; then it is back,
brighter—then gone in an instant. Over and over
this certainty dissolves. Over and over it returns
brand new. I keep calling it the Garden, but
who knows who it really is!

My foot settles in the mud on the path.
If my mind makes it mud, immediately
green grass and daisies appear. If I make it
green grass, it becomes dry dirt and
gravel. If I try to hold tight, all of
it fades away.

Garden of Gardens, always my teacher!
Mother of Mothers, you are the balm of my soul.
Lover of Lovers, intimate as no other!
Destroyer of Fear, Bedrock of Strength,
Fountain of Eternity—our Being Ungraspable:
World, without end.

+

In the darkness before
dawn,
a single bird
begins to
sing.

+

FURTHER IN

1

The cup drops to the floor,
the red wine runs and drains away.
Milk flows from breast to suckling lips;
new life in old containers will not do.
Each breath, the world entire,
is made anew.

The wind blows around the edges
of the house, sand drifts around corners,
a small grey squirrel races up a tree.
Nothing is going on anywhere. The
relief of release, of ceasing to be,
is a bliss and a blessing.

The earth revolves around the sun.
The moon revolves around the earth.
Morning to night my life orbits this beingness
of *me,* this knowingness of *I.* Atom
to atom, we cling to each other.
And who are we *all?*

Action or inaction? Movement, or
staying still? A force pulls upon me, but
I cannot see it; it is so far distant. Yet I swing,
pulled around its attraction, rolling into I know
not where, through the endlessness of space,
toward a green iridescent jewel.

2

I am in a boat, rocking on sparkling
blue-green water. My arm drifts in the ocean as
I gaze out to the horizon of the sea. Gulls
float overhead, their cries joining the
rhythmic splash of the water, echoing
the beating of my heart.

I wander the bluffs of an island.
Brilliant white sand meets impossibly
verdant green. My sandaled feet carry me
aimlessly along the edge of the sea. I lie
in the long grass, feeling the wind,
wondering where my goals have gone.

Down a path I find an abandoned cabin.
Opening windows and doors, I relax on the porch
in the shade. Inside, books rest on their shelves,
watercolors and brushes lie beside heavy
white paper on a mahogany table. A breeze
lifts the awning, then relaxes.

As evening approaches, I feel my neck,
my furrowed forehead relaxing. How many years
have I pushed and planned, forcing my way forward?
Is it possible to live without agenda? Can I exist
without tomorrow? The moon shines on the
cabin, on the old man asleep.

3

I am no age, neither old nor young.
My wrinkled hand is a crisscross of lines,
a network of reticulation. Brown spots
mark my skin, my hair is silver white.
Yet I was born this morning,
only hours ago, in the blink of an eye.

My breath carries me like the swell of
a wave—I lift and fall with the gentle rocking
of moonlit water, this motion of no motion,
the breath of the inward sea.
How old am I? How old are the stars?
Why do I even ask these questions.

Inside this beingness I am as young as each
new day, as fresh as morning's eye, as every
awakened ear. This touch, this taste, this newly-
met-you—where have you come from? Where
could you ever go? Where am I now, as my eyes
close, as the World slips into sleep?

Yesterday, a pain in my left ankle. Today,
an ache in my right toe. Only a blind person
could not see I am an old man. Only a child knows
what I feel inside. So much fills this small human
bucket. Let's play in its water, before it tips
over and we all spill out.

4

This morning the Dead visit me on
the veranda. We drink strong coffee and
watch the wind raise white waves on the sea.
The Dead do not like to be called the dead.
"That is a word the so-called Living use," they say.
"We are the ones alive, the ones who are real."

The sun shines through my companions. I cast
a shadow; they do not. *"We are so much clearer than you,*
like pure water, like crystal." If I blur my eyes they
are there, I can only see them with my heart.
They are complete like a jewel, like a chakra,
a whole life from beginning to end.

Later we go exploring together, up and down
the sandy paths by the sea. *"We are beings*
as you are—as are the trees, the animals, the clouds
in the sky." And where do you live,
I ask them? *"We live here, in this World,"*
they say, *"where else could we be?"*

In the evening I gaze over the palms and orchids,
over a glistening vibrant sea. Everywhere I turn,
living beings look back like raindrops, sands
cast up by the sea. Their vibration is endless, like
looking through rippled glass. We are one
multiplicity, unnumberable, inseparable.

5

The clear morning has turned spring
cold again. The rose quartz warms me,
and I feel the tension between the
old knowing of me, and that wide open
emptiness between one thing and
another, where I used to be.

I am in the pendulum swinging:
here, the knower known; here, the
swing into unbeing—the way one slides
down into sleep, sleep that is the hand
releasing. And you gratefully let go,
into no-thing-ness like a kiss.

Waking feels, after the amazement,
like a betrayal—living now in the I, and
of doing, of acting, as though things really
were. I feel my resistance, my subtle fear.
If I create you I will love you. And
then I will have to let you go.

I carry compost in bags to the garden.
Speared trilliums penetrate the air, bees seek out
the first flowers. I have grown used to ice and
grey skies—a residue of my mother's mother.
The sun breaks through, and with no
complaint, ice changes back to water.

6

The day rises into May, and through
the moist grey light warmth arises.
I wander through my old friends,
their young offspring succeeding them—
the daffodils and tulips, the trillium
and wild violet.

"So much like your mother," I say as
the bees nudge the pollen. *"I knew your
great-great-grandfather,"* I whisper in the
redbud's ear. Wandering in the Garden, I greet
the return of everything—the long slumberings,
the new arrivals, the bright open eyes.

"Where will I go?" follows me through the garden.
I think of my children, and their children,
wandering in the world. It is this *knowing*,
this being, that doesn't want to leave,
that wants to watch the sunrise, to feel
the spring rain season after season.

Eye near the ground, I watch ants and spiders,
a cricket sings near my ear. I am *this* close to earth—
I could sink and be inside her; I hold the flowers
as they drift from year to year. I am all
I hold outside me—I will leave the world,
and be right here.

7

It is early May in the Garden. Spring
has arrived late and the days are still cool,
the buds on the trees only now beginning to open.
Raised beds need turning but the ground
is all mud, full of water. The grass is green
and tall, yet too wet to cut.

Shifting from inside to outside is difficult.
The sky is so wide, the unruliness so deep.
Everywhere I look something needs doing:
hedges to trim, paths to repair from the deep ruts
of the deer. Piles of brushwood and broken
limbs rise like mounds of the Dead.

How can I balance this doing and non-doing?
My great love, to watch clouds form
and dissolve in the deep blue sky. Once
I get working, momentum carries me along—
but starting is like my chainsaw: pull
after pull and no spark.

I am Aesop's grasshopper: I fiddle and
loiter a whole summer away. There is some
kind of ease that toil seems to sunder,
and those who love working would of ease
say the same. I hold my hoe and fiddle
as the garden calls my name.

8

I sit on a marble bench in the garden.
Arranged by my side are clear stones of
ruby and emerald, diamond and topaz.
Each day I dig more; I clean and
display them, their inner light
their own sun.

After a misty rain, I prune and shape
the roses; I loosen the earth and remove
the weeds. Each movement releases their
fragrance, and my eyes sink into their
red velvet. A golden beetle climbs
in and around sharp thorns.

Wandering beneath the pines and locusts,
the wind sings a music of birch leaves and
wild grasses, goldfinches, and the wings
of countless wrens. White clouds race high in
the sky, and my soul tumbles into the grass,
into the yellow strewn dandelions.

What is there to do with all this beauty?
Shall I make an outdoor museum, label the
species, give guided tours? The silence
of the garden gives me the answer, and I
sink into the sounds of early evening,
the evening stars, rising within.

9

Today a brush fire of anger spread through
the garden. Grasses and old weeds burst into
flame; no matter how hard I beat back,
anger outran me, a roar of orange
flame and billowing black smoke. And
I the one who lit the match.

A disaster everywhere: beauty blackened
into ash and curling smoke. Burnt branches
crack underfoot, the roses lie scorched
and limp on the path. My sorrow is endless,
my senseless ways so repetitious. I sit
on the ground, sobbing.

In the morning I begin again, wearing
a black sash of repentance. Raking and
shoveling, I save what I can. Some
miracle has spared most of the roses;
the gemstones, while dirty, are stronger
than the heat of any fire.

Is there an end to the cycle of ignorance?
Are compassion and forgiveness truly
without end? The garden is healed by
the loving heart of the Gardener.
I sit in the rain, praying he too
can heal me.

10

After the fire burned away, I wander
in the dark earth-ash, blackening
my feet, raising dry dust into the air.
Everywhere I look are the stumps
of men, the burnt old ways, the
uselessness of toys and distractions.

My pockets are filled with the love of
before, round seeds from the Garden, hard
and dry. Between my finger and thumb, it
seems impossible these shriveled stones
could blossom into softness, could
turn a hard heart to love.

Dragging a stick, I furrow the black
and ashen earth, dropping my seeds
one after the other. I fold the earth over.
I offer a blessing and a prayer.
The night's soft rain whispers to wait,
to sleep in faithfulness.

On a morning when I had forgotten,
when the wind wandered in my hair and the
horses ran wild on the hill, there they were,
uncapped and blinking in the sun, uncoiling,
climbing into the air, my green children, on
their journey back from the dead.

11

A week of warm days and rain has restored
the garden. I wander off the paths, where
fire burned away brush and dried weeds.
Tiny blue flowers—forget-me-nots—shine
up with their round yellow eyes. None
of them remember last week's hot wind.

Incomprehensibly, the garden forgives
everything. What comes here is what comes—
wind, storm or snow. *"Whatever you are
is what you are."* murmurs the stream, whispers
the wind-blown grass. *"We are loved as we are,
you are loved simply as you."*

I am washed clean at the basin of the fountain.
The waters cascade over the rim, flashing
the brilliance of the sun. What is old, what
is carried as regret, as remorse, is washed
away. I shine like the new leaves of the birch
and willow; I flower into my Self.

My breath joins the breath of the wind.
I breathe the world into my being.
Gliding over the field on the hawk's wings,
I release the bones of old memories, the
paper-thin history of *me*. The soaring sky
kisses the horizon: all I look upon is new.

12

This morning I walk with my mother in
the garden: she is Mary, Mary Elizabeth.
She is Beatrice, Tris, the mother of my wife.
She is Barbara, the Red Rose, teacher of the
open heart. Our love flows unimaginably;
currents in the air, weaving heart to heart.

I ask her of the utterly other, of beings
and things that seem outside and apart.
"Like us?" she asks, *"We who have appeared
from your heart?"* I sit by the fountain
confused. My mother sits beside me
and strokes my hair, my shoulders.

Looking behind me, the mothers have
dissolved. I feel their love, no different
than my own. They leave a gift, a red box
tied with gold ribbon. When opened, a
hummingbird flies out, then returns,
to hover near my heart.

At dawn, the hummingbird leaves seeking
nectar. She returns to tell me of each flower,
butterfly and bee. At night she rests uncaged, in the
safety of my heart—her tiny wings folded; she is
the intimacy of me. Her iridescences are my
mothers, our love in the world.

13

This morning I ask the garden, why do I
want more? Greener needles on the pine,
brighter blossoms on the cherry? As though
what is were not enough, as though each
offering were refused, every gift being
not as great as what tomorrow might bring.

Last night's thunderstorms linger as broken
clouds and overcast skies. The wet grasses
and leaves have washed clean the song
of a single bird. Wet tires on the road,
the cock's crow: these are what the garden
whispers. These are its true words.

My old ways follow me, like the tangled
growth, the thorns and brambles of the
garden. I prune for beauty: the garden gives
me its wild ways. *"There is nothing
wrong with your desires; all we prohibit
are your prohibitions."*

I float on the green grass as on a calm sea;
below, tiny workers dig in the earth—above,
birds, bats and butterflies weave a net
to catch the stars. Someone has tapped the
flow of my anxiety, and it turns brilliant
and alive in the night air.

14

Yesterday's rains flooded our old damp
cellar. Little fountains of water sprang from
the cobblestone walls; in twenty-five years I've
never seen so much water. Rushing around,
renting a pump and hoses—the Garden sat out
there in the rain, hazy and unseen.

Now that the basement is pumped and
the sun has returned, I slosh through sodden
fields looking for the garden. In the basement
I rescued a small red squirrel, soaked and
shivering, and released him outdoors.
Today, I feel just the same way.

I sense the garden all about me, yet
I do not see it. When I am on the move,
everything moves as well. The horizon stays
distant, further away and out of sight. Some
inner dark worm is telling me it's not here—
yet I absolutely know it is.

Refusing to move, the Warmth surrounds me.
Standing where I am, the wind calms me down.
Voices of stones and trees reassure me, leaves do
a slow dance, inviting me to join in. Under my
feet, little rivers move in the grass. Each
thing that is, welcomes me home.

15

The Garden wants a summer house,
a pavilion of the alone, a place to welcome
the beauties of the garden. I see its
eight sides, the low spindled railing,
a curved and golden roof
that touches the sky.

Reading from my plans, I dig post holes
for the foundation and measure wood for the
pillars and deck. All day long saws buzz and
hammers bang; the smell of pine resin
hangs in the air. By evening its silhouette
stands black against the red sky.

This morning I paint finials and
move chairs and table onto the deck.
The shade in the midday sun is a blessing,
the view into the hills one of great relief.
Birds and nature spirits gather about;
the Dead linger, relaxing on the steps.

Welcome, I say, to all those gathered
around me. Welcome I say, to the
Silence, the emptiness that fills all things.
We raise glasses of wine in dedication,
to our discussions and debates, to our
joy-filled presence together.

16

An overcast day. I walk in the garden
before the rain, understanding the source
of my week's long malaise—I am longing
for the emptiness, the *Absence,* that underlies
the Garden. Looking down, I find the
entrance to a cave.

A key lies in a niche beside the ivy
covered door. It is invisible to anyone who
does not know it is there. Pulling up
from the ground, the door opens to receive
me. Lighting a candle, I descend step
by step into the earth.

At the bottom of a rough stone
stairway, crystals rise over me. I raise
the candle above my head and and starlight
sparkles away into the distance. The silence
is immense, the jeweled emptiness
goes on forever.

Here is what I longed for, unknowing. This
rich darkness, this jeweled earth, deep within
the Earth. The Garden above is filled with
immense beauty, yet without *this* beauty,
it is a hollow shell. The warm darkness
enfolds me, and I blow out the light.

I sit in the darkness, in the womb
of the Earth. Here, the silence is complete:
the non-existence is echoed by the clear
crystals. I fill with *nothing-at-all,* the
way a camel drinks at an oasis, the way
a breathless man breathes air.

All about me, the crystals reflect
the blackness. Formed without light,
they shine with emptiness, they bring
absence into radiance. From non-being
I am enlarged by infinity, my self
is dissolved into darkness.

Within the darkness there is no time.
Eons may have passed. I know nothing;
all is satisfaction, all is fulfillment.
From *no-thing-ness,* a hand strikes
a match: a hundred-thousand candles
flicker into brilliance.

Light is a stranger here. It brings what
is not into being. Climbing the stairs I return
to the garden. I close the earthen door, I replace
the key. The Garden, my very body, rushes back
into being—joyful for the evening sky,
for the light that creates the world.

THE ANGELS

1

Unable to sleep, I wander in the
garden. The paths are lit by the moon
and even the wind is silent. The night air is cool,
the grass is wet with dew. I am comfortable
being alone, and yet feel a longing for others,
for the nearness of companions.

The spring flowers, the tree blossoms,
exhale a fragrant presence, an essence of
pure being. These draw near in the dark,
their form luminescent, their touch intimate
and loving. They are kindness itself,
their caress, a warmth made of air.

"We are the Angels of the Night,
here to guide you and instruct you."
They gather as wisps and veils, the play
of light and shadows; shapes of beauty—
in the forms of beloved women,
of honored men.

"We are the garden grown as an
answer; we are your own wisdom, displaying
yourself to your self: opening your eyes
to what you yet can be." So I wandered
back to my bed. So I fell asleep
with you, Angels of Me.

2

Today the garden is flooded with perfection.
The panorama of greenness, the cool breeze,
the warm sun. Sounds are a nectar: the
chirping birds, the rustle of dancing leaves,
even a neighbor cutting grass. Everything
is in place, each moment a whole world.

In love with this moment, I invite the angel
to join me. His wings fold upon his back, like
a grey goose, a wild swan. His presence causes
no ripple in the world—he emerges as
presence. He sits shimmering, arms folded
on his breast; light, soft like the breeze.

"Your desire for me lets me fill you. You
empty, so I may arrive. We meet by becoming,
in you, what you think you are not. In this
way you are the field, the tree, the blue sky.
In this moment I am most fully present;
by your withdrawal, I Am."

Stay with me, I say. His reply is my own:
"We are Angels of Everything, arising
through your relaxing. We are the entry of
possibility, the flower of the death of the
closed door. We blossom where each
disbelief dies."

3

The angel sits in peace; she is quiet, her
inner activity is being. With her closeness,
I fill. She gives nothing but my own arising,
her radiance—my resonance. Her purity—her
purposeless purpose. Struck, her note of
pure being becomes my vibration.

She seems to arrive without, here where
we sit, watching the garden. She sits *there,*
yet arises *within,* manifesting from me,
simply because there is no *other.* We are joined—
she, the greater than I imagine, sprung from
whom is greater than she, than I.

A rainfall casts rainbows, our faces
are clear color, from visible to invisible.
Birdsong is the bliss of simplicity, the ordinary—
the hidden choir revealed. Waves move
between us, we ride waves of love,
pushing out over the wine-red world.

By my chair I gather my books.
Where is the angel? Where am I? This
rustling at my back, this sudden lift!
Who looks upon the world, the light spreading
over the field, the first stars nearer than ever,
as wings swim on the comfort of air?

4

I walk in the garden with the angel.
She walks beside me, to my left, to my
right, before me or behind. I walk with, or
within. She is my greater expansion—devils
are my contraction, my collapse
into the tightness of me.

Wherever we turn, radiance proceeds;
us-ness, being-with, brings joy to our hearts.
We are the lovers of our time and space—
we are two fountains merging,
bright water sparkling into
one tumbling flow.

We float among the lotus, we lie upon
the lily pads. White clouds in blue sky
are our wedding gift, we who have rushed
through constellations to each other.
Bells ring in the wind, flower
petals drift in the warm air.

Which was the outer, which was the inner?
Both are the blessedness, the weaving, the
one. Our eternity this instant, of lover knowing
lover—each the beloved, each lover the
loved. We walk with no substance,
we leave no trace but the dew.

5

Awake early, I am called by the earth
as by heaven. Here before the world wakes
there is inner quiet in the outer: the
rise of the hill, the patient presence of
the trees and grass. Is the breeze slow? Are
the birds' songs gentle without reason?

Slowly I am a sponge soaking up, dry sand
becoming moist. The garden began as
something small, the size of my room.
Now it spreads over hills and valleys,
acres of intimacy, mother to all,
a green vessel, a sustenance.

If I cannot see you—Angels as you are,
pictured by books, by unbelieved stories—
then I ask, *are you here?* And my
knowingness says *Yes,* for I feel you
as each beloved is felt, by the eyes,
the warm arms of the heart.

So many are gathered around, unseen—
endless though unhindered, uncrowded:
infinite space for infinite beings. Wherever
I turn I am lifted. In every falling I am caught,
in every hurt I am healed, every love is
returned with greater, brighter love.

6

The humidity and heat have relaxed,
and the garden is refreshed with coolness.
Why do I so love the Garden? Everywhere
I look, my eyes fill with love and with wonder.
I feel caring and community from every
leaf, dry stick, or stone.

As the wind blows I do not see hills or
trees or flowers. The creek no longer flows with
water, nor is the path lined with stones. The horses
on the hill are no longer horses, the birds in
the sky or sheltered in the trees no longer
sing with the voices of birds.

I see only angels—all are the
presence of the dead; life which is love
which is radiance rises from every existent
thing. Nothing is dead, not the ashen rocks
of the moon, not the crumpled
tin of a can.

So the angel speaks: *"We are the being
of every single thing. We are one, we are
uncountable. Why would we come as something
other? We have stood by you since birth as what
you love in the world. Earth, sky and wind—
would you love anything less than angels?"*

7

Today angels emerge from everything—
the tall grape iris, the white cascade of honey
locust blossoms. Even the grey weathered boards
of the shed—each essence shines with its
particular distinction; the iridescent
beetle flares green in the sun.

Brother Sun, Sister Moon. So Francis named
the angels—little brother, greater brother—
some tiny, some terrible in their immensity. Yet
here all sing one song, unable to see separateness.
Grasshopper lectures Crow, who advises
the towering Pine, the Eagle King.

When the realm is in order, heaven is above,
earth below. Angels, by being, spread peace
within the heart, within the whole universe.
"We are a wine of oneness, each what we are,
each a particular thing—an orchestra
of love being love."

Are You, world, the answer to my asking?
Are angels, are the dead, the entire fabric of
the world? My eyes are disbelievers, save for the
astonishment of Beauty. But my heart knows
and feels the arms of receiving, the joy
that rises into tears.

8

Everything fell out of thingness, and
overnight—gift of the stars!—arose as angels:
Angel of the Blue Sky, Angel of the White Clouds,
Angel of the Cock's Crow, Angel of the
Three-leafed Clover. Angels bloomed on every
breath—each beingness an Angel.

So slid away the dead world, the world of
the dis-connected, the piece-meal piece, unloved,
a separated *thing,* though each longed with their
heart's one song to return, *to belong*—and
their song was received, their grief
gathered and made whole.

Under the cover of dew, of grey dawn's
first particle of light, they returned, the infinite
uncountable, settling into each particular thing—
its beingness, its Angel, its shining light of
Aliveness, its radiation of hope, its beatitude
of unrelieved Beauty.

And my soul, my sinking stone, first to fall,
dragging the old empty separation behind me, a trail
of black burnt stars heard in my sleep their song:
the true Angel's Choir of the Earth singing
to me, calling me back, turning me round—
and I heard—and I came.

BEING IN THE GREEN WORLD

1

And so the world's words woke me up,
I who slept in my own mind, through
its miraculous greenness spread out with
no end, no seam, no stitch of top to bottom,
as it rolled like a wave made out of
morning song, and I drowned into life.

The soft wind carried a thousand summer
voices, each in a hush, a gentle giving way,
letting themselves be lost into distance,
polished by the tops of trees
and the pollen of oats, settling like a bee
into blossoms, into my welcoming ear.

The blue space of sky pulled, stretched
me open and thin, upward as I sat, solid
in my chair, feeling my head porous
and unresisting, toward lit particles of blue,
to lightness of space saying soundlessly:
love, love, love.

Waxed buttercups blaze in the grassweed.
The world wants me the way the river
wants each raindrop, the high way to come to
the low down, to travel—all of us—together,
gathering more and more as we go, until we are
gone, we are swimming in, we are the sea.

2

If you know what I will say before I say it,
I have failed us both. The day spins out of green
aliveness with no history—sparks from a wand
of fireworks, smoke fuming into whorls, lifted
by invisible pathways in the wind, like
currents of cream in coffee.

So the garden, while most present—filled
with lavender iris, covered in red-edged wild
rose—turns itself invisible, rises into the
floating world of aromas, making the air
itself sweet, and we breathe the beauty
unseen that flows over us.

It is as though I go out into my own wild soul;
the revealing earth bringing forth, presenting,
continually manifesting wonders, beyond
the capacity of one tiny mind to create—yet these
are all mine, emerging from me, not owned,
but in single multiflorous being.

The garden returns to solid ground. The sun
blazes overhead in yellow-gold intensity. My bare
foot feels each stone, each broken twig on the path.
Each step I climb higher. Each step I descend
into the earth. At day's end my body lies upon
the earth, as I sleep among the stars.

3

You who speak in your own way, in
your own voice green with the summer
wind, speak through me. My voice is your voice—
what have I to speak of, if what comes out is
not the world, the life of all livingness,
continually in birth?

My originality is only astonishment,
my being struck dumb by *your* being, which
is our being, born, moment by moment. This
you-ness of us—what I once sought to
imitate, to recreate. As though I was
apart, growing away from you.

My body broken bleeds blood— red rubies
and sapphires. My red wine is your green flowing,
streams of brilliance, of life; I breathe out flowers,
peonies transpire from my pores, landscapes lain
from my unfolding body, volumes of Earth
written in your words.

How I have longed to birth the world, even as
the earth births me, turning this body to
the inside of each green leaf, each tumbled stone,
singing—not *of* you but *as* you—world rolling
out from these eyes, these lips, these finger
tips, turning toward and into, you.

4

This one in me still struts, wanting to be
a god—while you, the whole world, gather
me in your arms, growing me into yourself.
We watch together as *this* morning displays
as mist and rain, as *this* afternoon breaks
through clouds into sunshine.

Magicians' tricks amaze the unwary; we
embrace deceptions, yet smile, knowing every
breath is a miracle, magic the constant state of
our being. Blossoms of clover, a tiny snake in
the grass, the hawk's glistening eye—appearing
and disappearing, moment by moment.

And where are we, watchers of the wide world?
Gathering this body, all we are left with is a bag of bones.
Within and without, we are unfindable; our nearest
kin, the space between the stars. No net catches
us, every weave is too wide—we who are
not, love our name: *invisible.*

Tiny raindrops tap on the roof of the tent.
The garden spreads herself, moist in the
grey morning. A neighbor hammers shingles
on his roof, each blow echoes, wrapped in birdsong.
A chipmunk runs back and forth in the grass,
owning the whole world.

5

One day you wake knowing *this* life—
the one you always tried to leave— is the one
you really wanted, the dream of your heart's desire,
and you are living it, breathing it into being, each
heartbeat your own life's love, beating as
a being held close to you.

Then fear rises, the fear that sent you
away, unable to bear the loss of that deepest
love—your own—that arose as the world.
But a hand took hold of you, strong, like
a father to a child, holding and lifting
you high, showing you the stars.

The secret, the key, was not one or
the other, not the emptiness of space, or the
galaxies of light, but how each held the other,
moving in and out of being, and the mystery
of love in the depth of non-being; how
everything grows out of Emptiness.

The branches of the locust float on the
evening breeze. The garden calls me back,
continually, like waves breaking on a calm shore,
as the sea scatters diamonds from the night sky,
then slides away, returning, all through
the night into dawn, into the new day.

6

The sun and morning warmth have
returned to the garden. Her presence is so
benign, so matter-of-fact, that I almost miss her,
she who is most in-factly here—as fish cannot
see water, as we who breathe air rarely
know the air.

Where I am, *whatever is* arises around me.
Summer paths in the garden, autumn leaves,
winter's brilliant bitter snow. I cannot predict
what the presence will be, other than what
is, moment by moment. Each arrival is a
new being, a blossom of my self.

Along the paths of the garden, off in the
tangled brush, high in the pollen-filled pine—
each is alive, in being *named*, in being *seen*.
Even the crow, stealing eggs from the robin's
nest, calls, *"I Am, I Am!"* This old body
blows away in the breeze.

The simplicity of the Garden wraps itself
around me. Or I, simplicity myself, flow into
and embrace every thing seen. Shadows and light
dance on the tree trunks. Blackberry sweetness
leans into the fourth of July. You and I
are the life of every living thing.

7

The garden is preparing for summer. It
relaxes and lays back, it welcomes the long
sun-filled days, the stormy wind-blown nights.
The days seem identical, and so the garden enters
eternity. Was it not always here? Though I seem
to remember deep snows, the bare cold winds.

Memory pulls me away, and the garden
hangs on, pulling me back to the present—
brilliant and distinct, filled with the certainty of
reality. Dreaming of the past or the future turns
me into a ghost; the garden wavers and
becomes hidden in mist.

Summer has turned languid. I wander
the mown paths without ambition, moving
from the shade of one tree to another.
Dragonflies dart through the humid air. The
light in the southern sky darkens, and thunder
rumbles in the distance.

After the rain the morning wind blows
down the hill with a cool breeze, with the smell
of alfalfa and horses grazing in birdsong.
I empty my pockets, my baskets of yesterdays
and relax with the newness, the nowness that
pours in with healing.

8

The beauty, the perfection of the Garden
is beyond understanding. After an hour,
when the tractor stops mowing, the silence is
like falling in a well. I hear the faint brush
of the willow's leaves, the legs of
a robin running in the grass.

As a child, did I go to Nature, to the
Garden, because I could trust you? Because
I *knew* you were Reality? You honored me with
your sunlight, with your birdsong, without
comment, without right or wrong. You let me
come and go, entirely as I pleased.

Showing me your treasures, you
showered me with gold. You discarded
everything you displayed, and in an instant
manifested more. My eyes became your eyes:
we watched together, we breathed
all of creation.

Now I reclaim what flowed outward into
Beauty. I am the receiver, the receptacle, the cup.
What I gave to others returns as my own. A golden
kingdom arises, built from my exhaustion.
The one who disappears, now returns as
Being, alive in the World.

9

Today I grow as the garden grows,
going nowhere, roots deep in the earth,
soaking in sunshine, drinking water and air.
I grow by being. I am intimate with insect
and bee, with birds and the deer. I grow,
I am consumed, I reappear.

I cannot speak from above. I must sink
below the earth, to speak from the depth
of resonance, through the roots of trees,
through schist and crystal, through stone.
I must be buried to know what earth wants,
to feel life's thick blood.

The old world rises up, as ancient oceans
raised the Himalayas. My past reemerges in dream,
an uptilted leviathan, titanic. I walk my childhood
streets, past the homes of old friends. I call to
my parents, who do not respond. It is
they who need call to me.

How many say, *"In the dark hour before
dawn."* Yet it is there I lose my way,
there I know, I do not know. The Garden lies
hidden in darkness, unfindable. I touch
the earth, I sit in the still place with
fear, and await the dawn.

10

These cycles of lethargy and joy,
of illumination and darkness—are they
different than sun and rain, than the bare
branches of winter, the green billowing
of a summer day? Do they mean more
than wind, less than rain?

I am a planet of trade winds and
droughts, cyclones and tornados, calm
winds on a flat sea. From Everest I see
the edge of the world, at the ocean's floor
none see me. I ride my universe,
turning through the stars.

I move among those afflicted with the
one way. Days of dark weather are my seasons,
no worse than light, no less desired. Even
the single day brings light and dark, and
who at midnight, entranced by the stars,
swears allegiance to the sun?

The rain has passed on. The Garden is
alive in greenness, more radiant from the rain.
The leaves move slowly, birdsong is dampened
and subdued. My feet leave a grey trail
in the grass, my pants and shoes
soaked with the morning dew.

11

Why would I make you something you
are not: leaf in a tree dancing, angel in the air,
whirling? Not either but both, not both but all—
everything that is. The warm air becomes
the baby's blanket; the separated earth—
the hand-maiden of hell.

Only-one-way, refuge of the terrorized,
trauma of earth not being solid beneath your feet.
The ease of the free-fall, the water-falling-down
dance of *this* changing into *that*, of form
relaxing into no-thing and forming
again, now and now and now.

Where are the sprouts of the garden?
Yesterday they pushed soil aside, raising their
bent heads. Today they are knee high to an
elephant's ear, green and glistening, loving
the burning sun. Tomorrow—*is there such
a thing?*—pregnant, about to birth.

Strange travelers: my young wife bends
into an old woman, thinning weeds and shoots.
Our kitten leaps into an old cat, still faster than I
out the door. The sky is as clear as blue water, yet
I cannot see the stars. The engine of a plane
becomes the song of an angel.

12

Ours is woven of the unendurable
and the ecstatic, the unbearable and
the brilliant, of simple love and selfish hate.
Ours is the weave of youth and beauty,
of worn and weathered deformation,
our vintages of wine.

His roving eye roams over, carried
like the wind, alighting, pollen on the
wind, drifting to and moving on, in and
out of beauty. *Her* beauty calls, unintending,
radiance ascending, in upturned eye,
the movement of the flower.

Their planes are an intersection, crystal
cleaved in new directions, being unintended,
neither her soul or his own. What moves,
this new amalgam? When my mouth
moves, your voice speaks; your
intention moves my hand, our feet.

At dinner, your grey hair, my split-ridged
finger nails. Our dimmed eyes clear as rain,
we sip a bitter brew. And as light breaks through
we touch and feel the warmth of inner air—
two mourning doves of softness grey, their
song a mellow loving coo.

13

Yesterday there was one, today there
are nine—orange daylily blossoms open wide.
This late spring emerged from a lingering
winter; the blackberries will not ripen before
the fourth of July. Yet now is never late,
now is always right on time.

Where are my own blossoms?
At seventy wild buds are bursting about me—
but in my tiredness, can I bring *anything*
to bloom? My old work was pinching off buds,
cutting away dead wood—but this season
has no need for any gardener.

This year I will grow wild and unruly.
Waving above the roses and begonia, I watch
deer graze in the upper field. Sweet fragrances rise
about me, I emerge unrestrained; love blossoms
as a flower. Butterflies surround me, bees
wander in the sweetness of being.

Wandering in the garden, what is
this new flowering bush? I did not plant it, I did
not see it grow! Yet here it blooms in resplendence—
yellow, gold and orange. Its color lights the
entire garden, the evening gathers
and basks in its glow.

14

Yesterday's summer storm has thrown
branches down everywhere, yet the morning
after is peaceful and calm. Last night in my
dreams I murdered an old colleague—
red blood was on his body, on the floor,
all over my hands.

The Garden allows both angels and demons,
the extreme ends of being. Summer reaches the shore,
yet the beach greets us filled with sharp stones.
Gliding on empty air, the eagle is caught only
when landing. We make our way through
jungles of darkness and light.

In the morning, breathing in, I relax
into our fuller being. My eyes open upon
the fields and trees, as one awakening from sleep.
I am filled with the air's cool breezes,
with the clarity of clear water; my dreams fade
into waking, into being, aware.

This is the relief of the Garden, the letting go
of the holding on, the contraction of fear. Each step
releases, each sight reveals the wideness we are;
each sound is our own sounding, each taste the
world's tongue. With each breath I am less in
aloneness—I become more fully the World.

15

The grey waves, the coming rain,
sweep over the hill, the hill waving its
dried oats, its alfalfa of mid August. The
horses answer the wind that races over
their manes, raising the tight hair on
their flanks, their glistening backs.

The wind moves the breath, the
being that arises into the past, into the
great sea of what was, stripping my bones
of their flesh, over and over, as it arises to
be *this moment,* this greeter of the new,
this love of the wind.

I paddle over the great sea of the Garden.
It lies below, just past my fingertips, wavering
in the sunlight, under the clear water. I watch
as I wander the paths below, as I tend
the flower gardens, as the fire burns,
as the phoenix is reborn.

The rain strikes the roof of the tent; the
boat bobs on the waves of the world under
the slate sky. Summer is doing it again—
packing up, getting everything ready to go.
But before then, storm or no storm, the
greeting: the whole love of the new.

AUTUMN LIGHT

1

It is a cool morning: the yellow squash
blossoms, the black-eyed susans are brilliant
yellow-gold in the sun. Here the seasons push
against each other; Autumn's fingers
stretch into August's summer,
feeling for a way in.

A grey hare races from the greens of the
garden. Out in the wooded hills, coyotes and fox
sniff the chill in the air, and wander the dry edges
of the field. Further back, reapers sharpen
their scythes, and in the far distance
an innocent child smiles.

The wind rolls the cycle of all things up
and down the hills, over the lakes and fields.
Grapes ripen on the vines, and satrys coax
the last nymphs to frolic in joyful nakedness.
I gather my pen, paper and ink, and begin
to trace the essence of the hills.

We are a small army, wandering these well
known paths: parents, grandparents, aunts and uncles;
strange warriors—artists and thieves, we bear the
bond of blood. Autumn will bring reinforcements:
first the scouts, then crunching through
the snow, *our triumphant dead.*

2

You, the Dead, do you call me, do you
gather around me? I see you through the trees,
the fields, the empty air. You stand behind,
unseen—yet gather close, felt as a crowded
denseness, behind my shoulders,
thick in front of me.

What do you want of me? For the
day still basks in emptiness, in high thin
clouds, in bird song. Everywhere is lightness
and freedom, yet I feel you silently
watching, waiting, like a
gathering storm.

Do you wait for *me* to join *you?* Now
that I know the beauty of the sunlit grass,
that is no different than my own? Or do you
gather to hear this music, this singing of creation?
For I am fully listening, and no one else
knows that you are here.

Or is this the absolution, that we gather,
dead and living, that allows us both to be?
Love's vibration in concentric worlds is listening:
I rest in your arms, O Dead; you rock me like
an infant, like a baby long away traveling in
the world alone, longing to come Home.

3

Late light lingers before leaving:
a gentleness ends the day, flowing across
the field, over and down my body. It has no
touch other than caring, *soundlessness* its caress.
In form, it would be *she;* in spirit, she
would be *your* eyes, loving.

Morning. I awake from the cocoon of
myself, and am inside the trees, within the
speech of green leaves dancing to birdsong.
A white cloud grows like an opening
rose: white angels expanding
in softly falling silence.

I have no need of miracles: *the gods
are immanent,* moving on the breath of
the wind. I am within the treasure-house
of everything: light creates dumbfounding
beauty, my own body hosts infinities of
pain. All being is my being, my body.

Circling, two huge woodpeckers alight,
one on each side of a pine. They peck holes
right next to me: their red heads, their black feathers,
their spotted breasts of white. Their cry is an
astonishment, and the fragile world
breaks open into Light.

4

The Garden wants to be uncontained—it
struggles against enclosure, like an animal
upon a leash. It thrives on losing borders,
on its ability to move in any direction. Rules
and borders are its death, and so, choosing
life, it continually outruns them.

The brilliance of the flowers, their yellow-
gold—pulled from the earth and given back
to the air—travel instantly, a beam directly into
my eye. Their fragrance diffuses the air over
great distances; bees and birds hear the
message and arrive from afar.

The Garden gives out everything as autumn
approaches. *Holding back* is only in our mind;
the green unfoldment knows none of it. When we
wish for more, it is only we who are constricted.
The sunflower reaches the sky as soon as it
births through the earth.

Everything is pouring out as it always has.
Autumn receives it, winter works its mystery
of returning all to emptiness. we ride on the surety
of the way things are: the morning sun, the cocks
crow, the familiarity of the breath. And then,
even when they are not.

5

The calmness of the eternal drifts
down over the new day. Late summer
extends her hand, and the sky is a clear blue,
the flowers shine with the inner light of the sun.
No thing lies outside this well being,
perfection is inherent in the day.

When I step out-of-doors the leaves rush
to me, tremulous in their speech, whispering
beingness. The barking dog, the crowing cock
enter immediately, leaving no distance
between us: they float upon the unseen,
coming forth, falling away.

The light moves as the sounds move, as the
leaves move, as the mind moves. It is a dance
of delight, an angel's veil lifting and falling,
barely revealing the beauty, the solidly known,
the softly seen, the foundation of the earth,
the love at the root of it all.

A falling leaf drifts and tumbles. Across
the field a white horse shifts her tail and
moves the breeze downhill. The sunflower
reaches high into the air, drinking in sunlight,
pouring out joy of being, emptying
herself into the World.

6

The Garden is the gateway, the way in,
the path to the innermost. The Garden is
the hidden center, the pearl hidden within the
defenses of the world. It can be reached by
ascent, it can be entered by sinking to
the innerness of everything.

This feeling of setting out at first
feels like leaving the Garden. But it
is a traveling *deeper in,* or *further out* into
the garden. It is as though a hole has opened
at our feet, and through it, our known
universe expands, unknown.

Are we descending into a well? Are we
climbing a ladder into heaven? All we know
is that in every direction what we see is
endlessness, the infinitely expanding,
the ever opening miraculous, as *what is*
keeps becoming *what is.*

Behind my shoulder the eastern sun
breaks through overhanging clouds. The
rays of the sun's light becomes the rays of
the sunflower's blossom becomes my eyes
streaming, feeding light into the sun; thus
all things, *in our brilliance,* shine.

7

The light through the overlapping
leaves sparkles like sunlight dancing
on water; the leaves and the air are aware:
their movement is our movement,
our great joy in being, in breathing
the blue air.

The Garden is overrun with excess;
pumpkin vines crisscross the paths,
colored gourds decorate the dry grass,
rivaling the colors of the summer flowers.
The leaves are thinning, and new space
enters with the crisp autumn air.

In previous lives contentment was
elusive; dark days followed bright,
and being in the world was a storm tossed
sea. Today's light and shadow are the
flavors of what is: salt and sugar,
musk, offal and perfume.

I find myself wandering in and out of
the garden; one minute on a leaf-strewn
path, the next in a car speeding down
the highway. Each moment's invitation
is to wonder: the ever-present,
presence of love.

8

I thought I could set you aside,
but you are before me, behind me,
and beckoning me ahead. You are my
mother's childhood blanket, my featherbed
of rest, my deep dark home, warm
in the texture of the Earth.

The Garden fades from a destination;
it is un-locatable on a map, it has no
boundary in earth or heaven. The garden
is built of snow and of starlight, of
moonflowers and the summer
light of the sun.

The Garden is miraculous: she strips
herself of everything in the orange light
of autumn; every leaf is shorn, every flower
falls. She pares herself down to barrenness,
to the hollow core of what we always
thought she was.

Yet her profusion has poured into
freedom; empty space pours out of
each dry pore. Where we were particular,
we are now far-seeing—releasing
what she was, all things become
potentiality: *anything can be.*

9

The sun rises beneath an egg blue sky,
the horizon of light a warm intensity
of golden cream, touching the turning
leaves and the bark of the dead pine
with orange incandescence—a fire
against the misted hills.

The garden is mist and fogs dispersing:
a grey-green offering to the goldenrod
and marigold. Above their shadows the
white clouds float in a brightening sky.
I am warm in my coat on a cool day
in late September.

It has taken me all my life to get here,
here where I always was, with morning
arising as blessing, within the welcoming
arms of the trees and fields. *"Have you
learned anything?"* they ask. *"To love
what is"*—my only answer.

Black boat on a deep black sea, I drift
beneath the stars in a moonless sky.
I lift and fall in the swell of the sea,
the stars turn above my head as I float
towards nothing at all, and in every
direction is morning.

10

The field makes all the difference: there
in the distance, pale and yellow-green; its
sharp edge an arc, bordered behind by dark
oaks and maples. So little is seen: the bushes
and trees hide most of it, but there the
horses run, back and forth in the sun.

The distance defines the space, it allows
what is confined by the close-up to open, to
fall away into depth; it opens a way to the clouds,
the deep sky, the stars. The sound of an airplane
pulls me further in; I fall deep into the
wavering drone, and disappear.

*We are fires, deep fissures erupting into
flame, we are rolling boulders and shrieking
ice, splitting into our aloneness and floating
away in the sea. We place our hands, our arms
over our ears, but we are shaken apart, we are
pierced by the grinding of sound.*

The field makes all the difference: it holds,
it re-stabilizes, it gathers what is distraught,
holding it firm in its solid sweep of light, giving
us Earth to come home to, after tearing ourselves
away, saying *"Settle in me and be relieved of
your striving. Sink into me and stay."*

11

We've spent so long—centuries—
grinding whole worlds to dust, that now,
when you come back as Beauty, you'll forgive
me if at first I don't trust, if I say *"Is this
deception?"*—looking at the locust leaves,
yellow, shocking the pure blue sky.

And the orange of this autumn,
remembered from one year to the next,
now as new as any new love, leaping up
from the green, holding hands with the depth
of beauty's dark eyes, that stare with no
hesitation, deep into mine.

Oh I am falling in love with leaving,
the verge of tomorrows here for only a
day, instants of everything pierced by arrows
of sweetness, dissolving this into that,
that into this, into freshness
refreshing forever.

Who were you yesterday when I watch
you today? Losing the *what-you-were* as
colored leaves drift away. Still the sun flares
on tangerine, dry wood's stacked to burn;
I am loving each yesterday, here now,
just beginning to turn.

12

Yellow birds, flocked to the earth,
fluttering to light, leaving to the air
her emptiness, as wind gives you leave
to land, brothers and sisters singing,
to the great green reception,
your welcome home.

Great space brings such joy, the
opening of the thick and heavy, the
beauty whose richness obscured, now
cleared—outbreath of the inbreath—to
breathe in without restriction, with
the freedom of the letting go.

So our angel unfurls her wings,
exultant in the wild air, beating as
breathing, lifting into the morning light—
soaring as walking, wide and wild, our
arms swinging, above and below
joined, one body beloved.

So I pick my way through the
Garden paths, past empty vines, under
the frosted purple grapes, hearing the
hawk's cry, seeing his wings soar,
knowing as my feet trod every color's
leaves, here I am in heaven.

13

The Garden releases its last
radiance, not as something failed,
but as its full reason for being: to give
continually, to its last bit of energetic being.
Its giving is its beauty. It is a smile,
it is the heart of love.

So the birdsong that surrounds me
is given, not away, but into the world.
It is given as rain, as sunlight, as snowfall
and autumn leaves. It falls on our ears
as *what it is,* with no deception,
the complete truth of being.

Even the smell of decay, drifting from
the deer, dead by the side of the road, says:
*"This is what I am and no other. I do not
pretend to be. Even in death I speak
without deceit, even unto my flesh,
my very bones."*

Be tolerant of these songs,
my musings on the way these things are.
For I cannot give up this Summer except by
giving myself as well, fully and completely,
into the praise of our mutual beauty,
our total loving of the World.

+

I am not dying away
from the world; I am
dying, one leaf
at a time, into its Beauty.

+

14

The pages of *The Book of The Garden*
flutter in the morning wind. So many similar
words, so many empty pages. Open this book
anywhere, and the whole world tumbles out.
The pen is in my hand, the white pages
beckon, the world says, *"Write me!"*

There is no way to stop. There is no
way to go on. Everything that is, appears and
disappears—clouds over the lake, moon after
the sun. You and I bring each other into
existence. The Garden is, when
I Am, when *We Are*.

I see a thousand other books. I see another
world, and another beloved sun shine. I see
gardens arise, like flowers by the billions.
I see your *knowing* of these worlds, identical
to mine. Our fingers touch across the
centuries, we sip the same wine.

Wandering down the path, the wild rose
snags my shirt. I stop and stare into the white
fragrant blossoms. Above, birds flit from branch
to branch. Every summer's sun reaches down
from the blue sky. The glow of sunset is
not an ending—*love is the only reason why.*

LIST OF POEMS

AUTUMN LIGHT